Forest Explorer

A LIFE-SIZE

FIELD

GUIDE

Nic Bishop

SCHOLASTIC PRESS ✦ NEW YORK

Contents

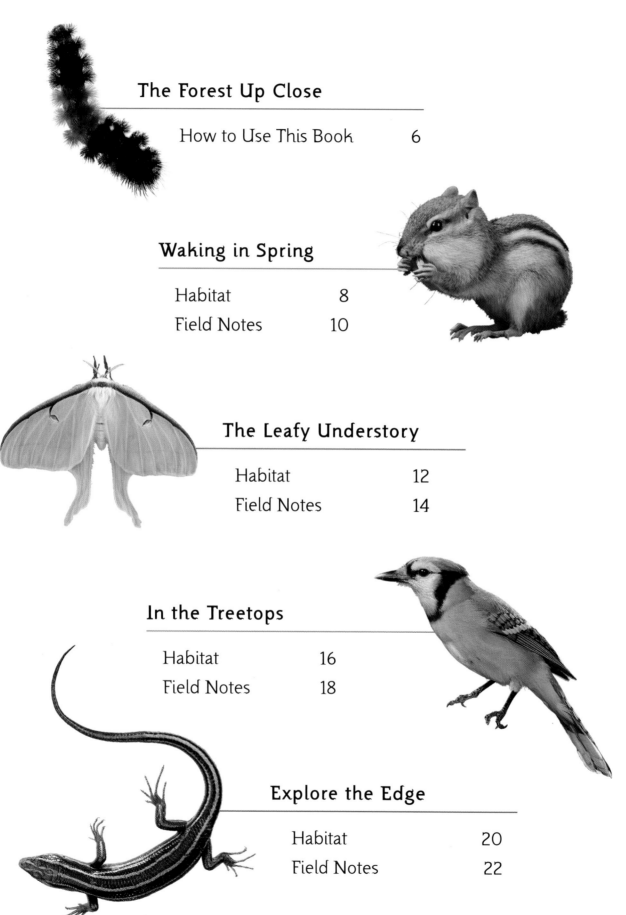

The Forest Up Close

Waking in Spring

The Leafy Understory

In the Treetops

Explore the Edge

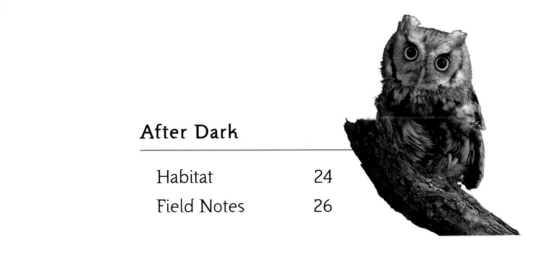

After Dark

The Fall

Winter Survivors

Be a Forest Explorer

Find That Animal

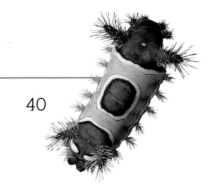

The Forest Up Close

HOW TO USE THIS BOOK

The forest is an amazing place, just waiting for you to explore. Beneath the treetops, hundreds of tiny animals are busy with their lives. Centipedes creep through soil, caterpillars crunch through leaves, and beetles hide in tree holes. This book will help you identify and learn about many of these creatures. Turn the pages to find more than 130 forest animals in seven big habitat scenes. They are shown in different seasons and in different parts of the forest, from the ground to the tops of the trees.

There is a lot to discover in these scenes. Take a close look and you will learn where different animals live in the forest and what they look like. Each one is shown life-size to help you recognize it in your real-life explorations. You will also see how each part of the forest has its own community of plants and animals that depend on one another for food and shelter. Many of these animals are shown hunting, feeding, hiding, or using other tricks to stay alive. Others are shown in different life stages, so you can see how they change as they grow.

After you have spied some creatures, turn the page. Field notes that follow will help you learn their names and find out more. You can read how these animals live in each part of the forest and how the forest changes with the seasons. You will discover how some animals hunt at night and how others survive in winter.

The forest shown in this book is called a deciduous forest, which means it's the kind that sheds its leaves in the fall. It's the forest that most people in North America will be familiar with. But don't worry if the forest near you is a slightly different kind. You will still find many of the same or similar animals shown in this book.

When you are ready to visit your own forest, turn to "Be a Forest Explorer." Here you will find tips to help you make your own discoveries. And don't forget to use this book to identify what you find. If you see an animal that interests you, turn to "Find That Animal." The picture index will help you find its name and where it is in the book. Have fun!

—Nic

forest layers

canopy

understory

forest floor

Waking in Spring

chipmunk

The forest wakes up in spring. Buds turn into young leaves and wildflowers bloom on the forest floor. Each new day brings more hustle and bustle as animals get busy with their chores.

baby katydid

Chipmunks come out of burrows where they have stayed for most of the winter and look hungrily for seeds. Baby katydids and tent caterpillars hatch from eggs. They are hungry, too. Katydids look for a favorite tree or shrub to eat. Look at pages 24–25 to see how much growing they have to do. Tent caterpillars spin silk nests like cotton candy in branches. They come out at night to eat leaves.

tent caterpillar

bumblebee

Queen bumblebees stir from a deep winter sleep inside underground hibernation chambers. Soon they are collecting nectar from wildflowers and looking for a place to nest. Bumblebees often build nests in old mouse burrows. Butterflies are on the go, too, visiting violets and other flowers. Spring azures hatch from chrysalises that have survived winter. Red admirals wake from hibernation as adults. Duskywings have slept through the cold months as caterpillars, hiding inside leaf shelters.

spring azure butterfly

red admiral butterfly

luna moth hatching from cocoon

Other animals are waking on the forest floor. The luna moth wriggles and scratches inside its cocoon. It oozes a liquid called *cocoonaze* to soften the cocoon. Then it cuts its way out with a special tooth on its body. The moth climbs a tree trunk to stretch out its new wings (see pages 12–13).

duskywing butterfly

The blister beetle crawls out of its winter den deep inside a bee's nest. How did it get there? When it was a tiny larva, the beetle hitched a ride on a bee and raided the

blister beetle

The animals you see here may be larger or smaller than life-size.

*pleasing
fungus beetle*

forest snail

harvestman

bee's nest for honey and pollen. The pleasing fungus beetle spent the winter
hiding under old logs or bark. As a larva, it grew up eating fungi.

*rove
beetle*

Soon you will find spring animals everywhere. Forest snails munch
decaying leaves — and sometimes other snails. Harvestmen, which are also called daddy-
long-legs, teeter on stilt legs. They eat dead things, but also grab small animals. You may
spot rove beetles, velvet mites, and earthworms under logs. Earthworms

*velvet
mite*

earthworm

can swallow their body weight in dead
leaves each day. A redback salamander may

be hiding here, too, waiting till night to come out and catch small insects.

*redback
salamander*

Along sunny trails you will find shiny green tiger beetles.
They run fast and have large eyes to see prey. Jumping
spiders have sharp eyes, too. They can spot a fly several
feet away. Then they stalk it and pounce with a sudden leap.

*green
tiger
beetle*

*jumping
spider*

The pesky dog tick feeds on blood. It clings to leaves and waits to grab
on to a passing animal. It could be a fox, a deer, or you. The tick hops on and
burrows in for a big meal. Deer flies sneak up from behind and land without
you knowing. Then they bite — hard!
blood. It gives her the rich food she
Male deer flies drink plant juices.

Only the female drinks
needs to produce eggs.

*dog
tick*

mayfly

deer fly

Many other animals are looking for mates in spring. Male mayflies dance
in glittering swarms near streams. They don't have long to attract females. Most
adult mayflies live for only a day or two. Hundreds of
spring peepers call to their mates near ponds. They make such a noise
you'll hear them a mile away. Later in spring, the toad starts its soft trilling
song. It's a very beautiful sound. When you hear it, you will
know that summer is not far away.

toad

*spring
peeper*

Turn back one page to see these animals in their true-to-life sizes.

The Leafy Understory

young red squirrel

The understory is the part of the forest between the ferns at your feet and the treetops above your head. It's the wrinkled tree trunks that stand around you. It's the twiggy bushes and young trees that brush your shoulders, and the old fallen trees that lie waiting to be explored.

By summer, when all the trees are covered with leaves, the understory is shady and sheltered. If it's hard to spot animals, listen carefully. Your ears will guide you. Squirrels and chipmunks run among bushes, scolding one another or looking for food. Some are youngsters that were born in spring. **Young red squirrels** make trips away from their nest when they are just seven weeks old.

red-spotted purple butterfly

jewelwing damselfly

Male **jewelwing damselflies** dance in sunbeams, showing their shiny colors to females. They are amazing acrobats. Damselflies have four large wings that help them hover in midair. If you spot what looks like a damselfly with antennae, then it's probably an **ant lion**. Their larvae hide in sandy soil and catch ants.

ant lion

wood nymph butterfly

A passing flutter of wings could be a butterfly, like a **spicebush swallowtail** (look for its caterpillars on pages 20–21), **red-spotted purple**, **wood nymph**, or **wood satyr**. Understory butterflies often feed on strange things, such as tree sap, puddles, dung, or even dead animals. It might seem disgusting, but these foods give them important nutrients.

Wood nymph and wood satyr butterflies use a trick to confuse predators. Round marks on their wings look like eyes. A hungry bird may wonder where the butterfly's head is, or whether it's a butterfly at all. The **eyed click beetle** is another trickster. It fools enemies into thinking it's a scary creature staring back.

wood satyr butterfly

spicebush swallowtail butterfly

Other animals have different tricks to deter predators. Anything that eats a **white-marked tussock moth caterpillar** will end up with a mouth full of scratchy hairs.

eyed click beetle

The animals you see here may be larger or smaller than life-size.

white-marked
tussock moth caterpillar

carpenter ants

arrow-shaped
orb weaver spider

The **arrow-shaped orb weaver spider** is too spiny to swallow. **Harvestmen** and **millipedes** taste awful because they have stink glands. **Aphids** use bodyguards for protection. They feed on plant juices and ooze a sweet liquid called honeydew, which **honey ants** love. The ants stay nearby and guard the aphids from predators like **lacewings**.

aphids and
honey ants

millipede

Check out a tree trunk to see how many animals you can find. Ants like the **carpenter ant** use trunks as highways to look for food in the treetops. You can't miss a **luna moth**. It is one of the largest moths in North America. In July and August you will find **empty skins of cicada nymphs**. A cicada nymph feeds on underground tree roots for a few years. Then, one summer it climbs a trunk and splits its skin. The **adult cicada crawls out** and flies to the treetops (see pages 16–17).

lacewing

Dead tree trunks have their own critter community. **Harvestmen** and **midges** sometimes hide in holes where it is damp and sheltered. You may spy camel crickets (see pages 24–25) sleeping under loose bark. Or you might find a huge **millipede**. Compare this one to the types on pages 28–29 and 32–33.

harvestman

luna
moth

midge

If you see small holes in the bark, that's a sign of wood-boring insects like **longhorn beetles** and **pigeon horntails**. A pigeon horntail has a long egg tube, called an *ovipositor*, to lay eggs inside old tree trunks. When the eggs hatch, the horntail larvae bore through the wood. That's if they aren't eaten by giant ichneumon larvae. When a **giant ichneumon wasp** lands on a tree, it feels for tiny vibrations made by a horntail larva feeding inside the wood. Then it pushes its ovipositor more than an inch deep into the tree to lay an egg in the larva's tunnel. When the ichneumon larva hatches, it makes a meal of the horntail larva.

longhorn
beetle

pigeon
horntail

adult
cicada
crawling
out of
nymph
skin

empty cicada
nymph skin

giant ichneumon wasp

Turn back one page to see these animals in their true-to-life sizes.

In the Treetops

giant swallowtail butterfly

Look up! The leafy treetops are a part of the forest called the canopy. Giant swallowtails and other butterflies soar among the branches high above your head. They may be looking for mates, or migrating to new forests. Some canopy creatures may be visitors, like the praying mantis that has flown from a meadow nearby.

praying mantis

Very small animals sometimes use the breeze to float through the canopy. Young spiders have a trick called *ballooning*. They let out silk streamers until the wind tugs them off their feet. Woolly aphids have long fluffy coats and drift like puffs of thistledown. They sail away to new homes.

ballooning young spider

woolly aphids

Birds swoop and dive through the canopy. Mostly they are looking for food or chasing neighbors. Sometimes they just seem to be having fun. The blue jay is one of the prettiest, and noisiest. It bosses other birds and copies their calls. But the loudest canopy noisemaker is the cicada. The males make all the racket. Some can be heard a quarter of a mile away.

blue jay

cicada

For caterpillars, the canopy is like a dinner table of tasty greens. From the time it hatches from an egg, the main job of a luna moth caterpillar is to eat and eat. It has to grow five thousand-fold before it is big enough to turn into a pupa.

luna moth eggs

luna moth caterpillar

mourning cloak caterpillar

A big group of mourning cloak caterpillars or gypsy moth caterpillars can eat so much they harm a tree. But that doesn't happen very often. Wasps, birds, and other predators help keep caterpillars in check. Some birds catch more than a hundred caterpillars a day when they have babies to feed. But they had better not touch a saddleback caterpillar. It has a prickly way to deal with predators — sharp stinging spines.

gypsy moth caterpillar

saddleback caterpillar

The animals you see here may be larger or smaller than life-size.

walkingstick

stilt bug

treehopper

Other canopy critters fool predators by making themselves hard to find. **Measuring worm caterpillars** stretch their bodies out like twigs. **Stilt bugs** and **treehoppers** have strange-looking bodies that predators may not recognize. The **walkingstick** is almost impossible to spot. When it moves, it rocks back and forth like a twig wobbling in the breeze.

measuring worm caterpillar

Some predators can be difficult to find, too. It's hard work to spot a **Brochymena bug** resting on bark. It eats caterpillars and other insects. The **robber fly** sits very still in a sunny spot, watching with large eyes. Then it zooms off to pounce on a passing insect. It might catch a **scorpionfly**, or even a big moth or bee. It stabs it with a sharp mouth and sucks the body dry. Ladybugs, like the **convergent ladybug**, hunt slowly. They wander along, snatching aphids.

Brochymena bug

robber fly

scorpionfly

convergent ladybug

Hundreds of different wasps hunt for insects to feed their young. The **cicada killer wasp** stings cicadas and carries them to its underground nest. It lays an egg nearby so its young can later eat the cicada. The **pelecinid wasp** lays eggs underground so its young can attack beetle larvae in the soil. Many **ichneumon wasps** lay eggs near beetle larvae that live deep inside wood. Scientists believe ichneumon wasps can taste with their egg-laying tube, or *ovipositor*. This helps them lay their eggs by just the right insect food.

cicada killer wasp

ichneumon wasps

pelecinid wasp

There are about three thousand different types of ichneumon wasp and more than sixteen thousand different types of fly that live North America. Scientists have only studied a few of these. Even many well-known flies, like **snipe flies** or strange-looking **stilt-legged flies**, have not been thoroughly studied. We still don't know for sure how all these animals live, where they lay their eggs, or what they eat. That's the exciting thing about being a forest explorer. There are so many mysteries to uncover.

snipe fly

stilt-legged fly

Turn back one page to see these animals in their true-to-life sizes.

spangled fritillary butterfly

Explore the Edge

The forest edge is a neat place to explore. You can find animals from both the forest and nearby meadows living side by side.

Watch meadow butterflies like **spangled fritillaries** and **American coppers** sipping nectar from wildflowers. Spot other creatures like **green tiger beetles** hunting in sunny spots. **Black bee flies** wait nearby. Their larvae eat tiger beetle larvae. Then just under the trees you will see forest-loving animals. **Wood frogs** hunt spiders and beetles. **Slugs** feed on decaying plants.

American copper butterfly

black bee fly

wood frog

green tiger beetle

slug

You may surprise a cottontail rabbit at the forest edge. They often hide here by day. They may raise their families here, too. **Young rabbits**, called _kits_, are ready to look after themselves soon after they are two weeks old.

Small tunnels in the long grass are a sign of **meadow voles**. These animals chew the bottom of plants to make secret runways. Then they can explore the meadow hidden from foxes and hawks. Meadow voles are always hungry. They can eat more than half their body weight in seeds and plants each day.

young rabbits

meadow vole

grasshopper

field cricket

The forest edge is also a favorite place for snakes. That's because there are lots of reptiles like skinks and sunny spots where they can sit and warm up in the morning. Yet it's easy for them to scoot under a log or bush if they are scared. The **five-lined skink** ambushes **grasshoppers**, **field crickets**, and other insects. It also has a clever trick to escape predators. If an animal grabs its tail — the tail falls off! The skink gets away and grows a new tail later.

The **brown snake** hunts worms and grubs. It has no venom, so it can't defend itself very well. But it can squirt a smelly liquid to deter predators from eating it.

brown snake

five-lined skink

The animals you see here may be larger or smaller than life-size.

worker termites

soldier termites

Old logs are a good place for **termites**. They look like white ants, but are more closely related to cockroaches. Termites live in large groups called *colonies*, which are hidden underground or in dead trees. They eat wood. **Workers** collect food and look after the young and the queen, which lays all the colony's eggs. **Soldiers** defend the colony. You almost never see termites in the open. The only time is when young, winged **king** and **queen termites** leave the colony. They fly off to start new colonies.

king and queen termites

net-veined beetle

Animals should beware of yellow and black-colored critters. These colors mean "keep away." The **net-veined beetle** has yellow and black stripes to warn birds that it tastes bad. The **elderberry longhorn beetle** may taste bad, too.

elderberry longhorn beetle

yellowjacket

bumblebee

spicebush swallowtail eggs

The colors of **yellowjackets** and **bumblebees** warn animals that they are stingers. But what about the **flower fly** and **robber fly**? They can't sting. They fool predators by looking just like yellowjackets and bumblebees.

flower fly

robber fly

young spicebush swallowtail caterpillar

older spicebush swallowtail caterpillar

Caterpillars of the **spicebush swallowtail butterfly** fool hungry birds by looking like something they wouldn't want to eat. The **eggs** hatch into **young caterpillars** that are brown, white, and slimy-looking. Just like bird droppings! **Older caterpillars** are green and have two large eyespots. These aren't real eyes. But they make each caterpillar look like a small snake.

These tricks may scare a bird, but they won't fool an **assassin bug**. Assassin bugs can't see as well as birds. They don't notice disguises and copycats. They just grab an insect and suck out its insides.

assassin bug

But an assassin bug had better not attack a **bombardier beetle**. It fires a jet of burning chemicals at its enemies with a loud pop. Even a hungry mouse will be sent running. The **click beetle** has a secret surprise, too. It flicks its body with a loud snap, to scare predators into dropping it.

click beetle

bombardier beetle

Turn back one page to see these animals in their true-to-life sizes.

gray tree frog

After Dark

crane fly

camel cricket

Many animals go to sleep when the sun sets. The chipmunk heads for its burrow. Cicadas stop singing, and birds fly to their resting places. But other animals wake up. **Plume moths** and **crane flies** flutter into the darkness. The **camel cricket** crawls out of a tree hole and climbs down to the forest floor. Mice run along logs, and toads rustle through the leaf litter. The night is just as busy as the day.

plume moth

brown prionid longhorn beetle

There are many reasons why animals come out at night. Frogs have damp skin that would dry out during the day. A moist night is perfect for the **gray tree frog** to hunt bugs in the branches. It may also be safer at night when many predators are asleep. The **dobsonfly** and **brown prionid longhorn beetle** are less likely to become bird food when they go looking for a mate. The **bush katydid** might not be spotted while it's munching leaves.

dobsonfly

Night is also a good time for a katydid to *molt*, or shed its skin. All insects molt so they can grow. That's because an insect's skin is hard and can't stretch to let it get bigger. When it molts, the **bush katydid** hangs upside down and steps out of its old skin. Its new skin is soft and damp. It stretches to allow the insect to grow quickly.

bush katydid

molting bush katydid

This is a dangerous time for a katydid. It cannot fly or run while its skin is still soft. And there are always predators on the prowl, even at night. The **screech owl** and the **opossum** love juicy katydids. The bush katydid has to stay still for almost an hour while its new skin hardens. Then it can go on its way.

screech owl

young opossum

The animals you see here may be larger or smaller than life-size.

flying squirrel

Night animals use sharp senses to find their way. Owls have large eyes to see in the dark. They also have ears that can pinpoint the tiny rustling of a mouse or cricket under the leaf litter. Opossums and **flying squirrels** have large eyes, as well as a sensitive nose and whiskers. Flying squirrels have furry flaps of skin that stretch out when they leap from tree to tree. They glide through the night, looking for fruits and nuts.

Insects have their own special night senses. Katydids and camel crickets wave long antennae to feel and taste their surroundings. **Mosquitoes** use antennae to home in on sleeping birds and mammals. Some can sense a person's body warmth and breath from one hundred feet away. Then they move in for a midnight feast.

mosquito

Moths use their antennae to find a mate. At night the female **cecropia moth** produces a chemical perfume, called a *pheromone*, which drifts away on the breeze. The male moth's antennae can pick up the scent from miles away! Then he follows the smell to find her. The **scarab beetle** and **brown prionid longhorn beetle** use pheromones to signal to their mates, too. These beetles lay eggs on old trees, and their larvae feed inside wood. You can see a scarab beetle larva on pages 32–33.

cecropia moth

scarab beetle

If you listen on a summer night, you'll hear how other animals signal to their mates. Katydids, frogs, and toads create a lively chorus of chirps, croaks, and trills. Each type of animal has its own song so it can recognize its own kind. The males do the singing to let females know where they are. Their singing also tells other males to stay away.

Male **fireflies** signal with their lights. Each kind of firefly has a special light signal, and when the female recognizes the right one, she replies with her own special signal. This tells the male firefly where she is. But it could be an ambush. Sometimes a different type of female firefly will copy the signal. She tricks the male into landing nearby. Then she eats him!

firefly

Turn back one page to see these animals in their true-to-life sizes.

The Fall

carrion beetle

Summer doesn't last forever. Slowly and steadily, the nights get cooler. One morning you'll notice the first frost sparkling on the ground, or the first leaf changing color. Then you know fall is on its way.

Each leaf that falls becomes food for litter eaters living on the forest floor. **Millipedes**, tiny **forest snails**, and other decomposers chew through the dead stuff. Millions of tiny jaws munch it into small pieces and mix it back into the soil.

millipede

forest snail

carrion beetle larva

When a mouse or squirrel dies, it, too, becomes food for decomposers. **Carrion beetles** home in on the animal's scent and lay eggs under its body. The young **beetle larvae** hatch and chomp through the rotting food. Flies lay eggs that hatch into hungry **maggots**. Then **rove beetles** arrive to munch the maggots.

rove beetle

It may seem horrible to eat dead things. But decomposers are very important. They are the forest's recycling crew. They make sure everything is chewed up and broken down. It all gets turned into nutrients that fertilize the soil and keep the forest healthy.

maggot

The most amazing member of the crew is the **burying beetle**. It can find a mouse almost as soon as it dies. Then it releases a pheromone scent to call a mate to help it. The two tiny beetles crawl under the mouse. They lie on their backs and use their feet to move it to softer ground. Next, they bury the mouse beneath the leaf litter so other animals can't find it. The two parent beetles then stay underground. They raise their young and use the mouse for food.

burying beetles

Lots of predators lurk in the leaf litter. **Rove beetles** snatch prey in their sharp jaws. **Spotted salamanders** catch earthworms and slugs on damp nights.

spotted salamander

rove beetle

The animals you see here may be larger or smaller than life-size.

*comma
butterfly*

*spider wasp (bottom)
and prey*

wolf spider

At night, the **wolf spider** creeps over the ground.
It feels for the vibrations made by crickets and beetles
rustling through the litter. Then it pounces. But sometimes a
predator becomes prey. During the day, the **spider wasp** flies and runs
across the forest floor. It checks every nook and cranny for a spider. When it
finds one, it paralyzes the spider with a sting and drags it to its burrow. The wasp
lays an egg nearby so its young have spider food when they hatch.

*Formica ant
and larvae*

Animals notice the arrival of fall, just as we do. They sense the cooler,
shorter days and start to get ready for winter. **Deer mice** look for seeds
and store them to snack on later. **Garter snakes** head to underground dens
to hibernate. They huddle together, sharing warmth and moisture. The
comma butterfly finds a hollow log to hide in. **Formica ants**
spend more time sheltering in their nests,
tending their queen and young **larvae**.

*deer
mouse*

On fall walks you will spot **woolly bear
caterpillars** migrating over the ground.
They are looking for hibernating places,
too. You may see **orange-striped oakworm
caterpillars** come down from the trees to
burrow into the litter. Each one
turns into a pupa (see pages
32–33) that will hatch in spring.

*woolly bear
caterpillar*

*shield-back
katydid*

*orange-striped
oakworm caterpillar*

Many other insects die at the end of summer.
Cicadas fall to the forest floor and become ant food.
Shield-back katydids die, too. But these insects will
have laid eggs that survive until next year.

*garter
snake*

dead cicada

Turn back one page to see these animals in their true-to-life sizes.

Winter Survivors

white-footed mouse

gray squirrel

Wrap yourself in a warm coat and go outside. The winter woods are a beautiful place for a walk. Icicles sparkle on bare branches. Fluffy white snow cloaks the ground. But for animals, this is a difficult time. It's very cold and there is almost no food. How do they manage? A few animals, like geese, robins, and monarch butterflies, fly south to where it is warmer. But those that stay behind need special ways to survive.

The **gray squirrel** grows an extra-thick coat to keep warm. It also has food, because it buried lots of acorns in the fall. You can watch squirrels dig up their nutty snacks from under logs or in old tree stumps. Perhaps a red-bellied woodpecker and a white-footed mouse will turn up. There could be a snack for them, too.

The **red-bellied woodpecker** can fluff out its feathers to keep warm. But it has a hard time finding enough food to eat. It may visit bird feeders for food. The **white-footed mouse** makes a special winter nest of leaves and feathers tucked in an old burrow or birds' nest. It keeps a store of seeds handy, but goes exploring for extra food.

sow bug

pill bug curled up

pill bug

owl pellet

It's dangerous to be a mouse. Take a good look at an **owl pellet** and you will see why. An owl pellet is a ball of fur, feathers, and tiny bones that an owl coughs up after a meal. With a magnifying glass you can check out the remains of what it has eaten. That usually includes mice.

You may find clues to how other critters survive by looking at where a squirrel has been digging. It may have disturbed some decomposers, like **sow bugs**, **pill bugs**, and **millipedes**. They normally

red-bellied woodpecker

millipede curled up

The animals you see here may be larger or smaller than life-size.

orange-striped
oakworm pupa

luna moth
cocoon

scarab
beetle
larva

hide deep in the litter where the frost cannot reach. The **orange-striped oakworm pupa** shelters here, too. The **luna moth pupa** spends winter protected in a **cocoon** made of silk and leaves. It spun the cocoon while it was a caterpillar (turn to pages 8–9 to see the cocoon hatch).

Wood eaters, like **scarab beetle larvae**, stay inside the dead tree they are eating. They know that the inside of a rotting log is a little warmer than the outside. Other insects rest under logs or bark. They may look dead, but they are just too cold to move or eat. They are in a deep winter sleep, waiting for spring to wake them.

woolly
bear
caterpillar

Some insects have an interesting way to survive the winter. They make a special antifreeze in their blood so they don't freeze solid. **Woolly bear caterpillars**, **mourning cloak butterflies**, **question mark butterflies**, and **ladybugs** do this. They hibernate in hollow trees and under leaves. You may even find them sleeping in your garage.

These insects can wake up on warm days, even before winter has ended. So don't be surprised to see a mourning cloak flying through the snow-covered woods on a fine day. When it lands, it opens its dark wings like solar panels and turns to the sun. The wings are very good at absorbing sunlight, and this warms up the butterfly's body.

question
mark
butterfly

bagworm
moth bag

pink-spotted
ladybug

Winter kills many other insects. But they survive by leaving their eggs behind. The **bagworm moth** hides its eggs in a bag made of twigs and leaves, spun together with silk. It made the bag to hide in when it was a caterpillar. It slept inside by day and poked its head out to eat leaves at night. When it became a moth, it laid eggs in the bag before it died. **Katydids** leave their **eggs** hidden in leaves and bark. Look through a hand lens and you may see katydid babies inside. They are waiting to hatch when the first leafy buds open in spring.

Asian
ladybugs

mourning cloak
butterfly

katydid eggs

Turn back one page to see these animals in their true-to-life sizes.

Be a Forest Explorer

HINTS AND PROJECTS

The woods are waiting for you to explore. Check out the tips below and start planning your own expeditions. You should be able to find many of the animals shown in this book. But remember — obtain permission from a parent or guardian before visiting a forest, and never go alone. You must always go in the company of an adult who will be responsible for you.

A favorite forest. The first thing to do is find a favorite forest to explore. It doesn't need to be big forest or one that's far away. Many of the animals in this book can be found in any patch of trees. Some even live in leafy backyards. The best plan is to find a forest that has good trails, lots of critter habitats, and expert rangers who can answer your questions. Check out nearby nature centers, wildlife sanctuaries, and conservation reserves. Some state and town forests also have good services.

Once you have found a place to explore, you will need an explorer's kit to help you observe nature. Take a pair of binoculars to study animals like birds and squirrels without disturbing them. Carry a magnifying glass for an up-close look at small critters, and a collecting jar to keep a beetle or bug in while you study it. Remember that you should never disturb or touch any animal unless an adult says it's okay.

blue jay babies

You may hurt it, or it could sting or bite. If an adult says it's okay, you can use a small brush to gently move an insect or other small critter while you study it.

A forest journal.

A good thing to take on your walk is a forest journal. This is a book in which to write your discoveries and thoughts. Here are a few things to note down when you make an observation. Write the date, time, weather, and place where you made the observation. This is very useful information. Perhaps you will want to come back to the same place one day. You may want to compare your observations in different seasons or in different weather.

a simple food chain

caterpillar eats leaves

bird eats caterpillar

If you find an interesting plant or animal, do a sketch and note down things like its size and color. Does it have wings and legs? How many? Does it have antennae? How long? Does it have any special markings, such as bright colors, stripes, or eyespots? You should also describe the place where the plant or animal was living. Was it on the forest floor? Was it on a tree trunk or a leaf? Lastly, write down what it was doing and what it was eating. This information will help you identify the animal later.

As your journal grows, you will learn more and more about the forest. Eventually, you will be able to recognize different trees by their leaves. You will learn the differences between groups of animals, like birds, mammals, insects, and spiders. You will know which animals eat plants and which eat other animals. You may be able to draw a food chain. That's a list of different living things that depend on each other for food. For example, caterpillars depend on trees for food, and birds depend on caterpillars for food. Thinking about food chains will help you understand how a forest works. It's made of many plants and animals that need one another to survive.

a butterfly pupa↗
is called a chrysalis

← a butterfly larva
is called a caterpillar.

Walking through the seasons. One of the best things about exploring a favorite forest is watching how it changes during the seasons. Every time you visit, new things will be happening. There will be new observations to write in your journal, new animals to see, new sounds to hear, and new mysteries to think about. Here are a few things to look for through the seasons.

March-April-May. Listen on warm damp evenings for wood frogs, spring peepers, and toads. Watch for the first spring wildflowers, then look for bumblebees and early butterflies feeding on them. Look for the first leaves to open. What trees do they belong to? See if you can find baby caterpillars and other insects that have just hatched. You may spot turkeys in forest clearings or hear woodpeckers drumming on tree trunks. Birds such as orioles, tanagers, grosbeaks, and wood thrushes may migrate to your forest from farther south at this time to start nesting.

June-July-August. As summer arrives, you'll see more insects. Look for dragonflies and large butterflies like swallowtails. Young birds and mammals that were born earlier in spring will be ready to leave their nests. Watch for young squirrels chasing each other and trying to establish their territories. Later, the insect noisemakers — crickets, katydids, and cicadas — will start their summer singing. Look for signs of animal activities. It could be some chewed seeds left by a squirrel or holes made in tree trunks by wood-boring insects. Try to guess what these clues might mean.

September-October-November. As it gets cooler, animals prepare for winter. Watch for squirrels and blue jays gathering acorns. What do they do with them? Forest birds have finished raising their young and some gather in small flocks, feeding on fruit and seeds in preparation for migration south. Write down when you see monarchs migrating and when cicadas stop singing. Which are the first trees to lose their leaves? Once the leaves have fallen, it's easy to spot old birds' nests. You will see old wasp nests in the bare branches, too, as well as the cocoons and pupae of moths and butterflies. Deer, foxes, raccoons, and other large forest animals are also much easier to see when the leaves have gone.

December-January-February. Look for animal tracks in the snow and try to figure out what the animal was doing. Was it looking for food? Was it escaping danger? Draw the tracks so you can identify them later. Check out a bird feeder at the nature center and learn to recognize the birds that live in the forest all winter. Visit the library to find out where the migrating birds you saw in summer have gone. Then draw a map to show how far these places are from your forest.

Glossary

antennae-the two feelers on an insect's head.
cocoon-the silk case that protects the pupa of some insects.
habitat-the place where a plant or animal lives.
larva-the young of insects such as butterflies, beetles and flies. (larvae-more than one larva).
nymph-the young of insects such as grasshoppers, cicadas and walking sticks.
pupa-the resting stage a larva turns into before it becomes an adult.

SAFETY FIRST

It's fun to visit the forest, but you should always be careful and respectful. Remember that even a small forest is a wilderness area. Always talk to a parent or guardian first, and always go in the company of an adult who knows the forest and will be responsible for your safety. Here are some of the commonsense rules you should follow.

1. Don't touch or disturb any animal unless a responsible adult says it's okay. You may harm the animal, or it may bite or sting. Bites and stings can be very serious for some people. Don't touch a dead animal.

2. Don't approach an injured or sick animal. Tell an adult who knows how to help.

3. Take suitable clothing and adequate water and snacks. Don't eat or drink anything you find in the forest.

4. Always stay on the trail. If you leave the trail, you may damage fragile plants or wander into unsafe areas.

5. Wear long pants and a long-sleeve shirt, and apply insect repellent to exposed skin. Some mosquitoes and ticks can pass on serious diseases to people. A parent or guardian should check you all over for ticks when you get home. They should seek proper advice about what to do if one is biting you.

6. Don't visit a forest if stormy weather or lightning is expected or if people may be hunting.

There may be other safety rules you need to obey in your particular area. A parent or guardian should help you find out about these. In any event, always have a responsible adult with you when you explore a forest. Have fun, safely.

Find That Animal

A PICTURE INDEX

The animals you see here may be larger or smaller than life-size.
They are shown life-size in the habitat scenes.

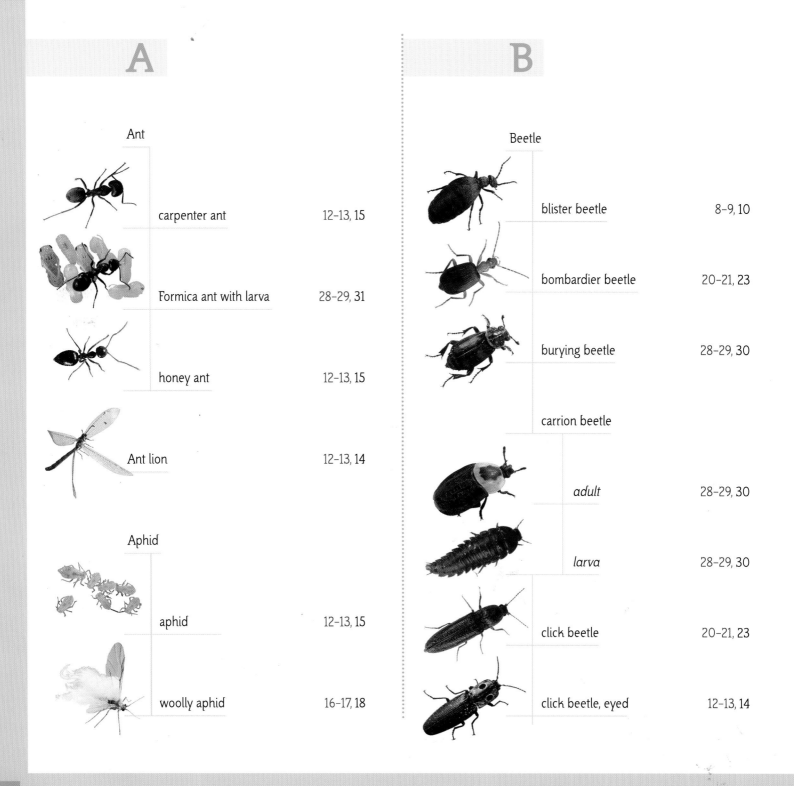

A

Ant

carpenter ant — 12-13, 15

Formica ant with larva — 28-29, 31

honey ant — 12-13, 15

Ant lion — 12-13, 14

Aphid

aphid — 12-13, 15

woolly aphid — 16-17, 18

B

Beetle

blister beetle — 8-9, 10

bombardier beetle — 20-21, 23

burying beetle — 28-29, 30

carrion beetle

adult — 28-29, 30

larva — 28-29, 30

click beetle — 20-21, 23

click beetle, eyed — 12-13, 14

*Page numbers in purple refer to pictures. Page numbers in **black** refer to text.*

firefly 24-25, 27

green tiger beetle 8-9, 11; 20-21, 22

ladybug beetle

Asian ladybug 32-33, 35

convergent ladybug 16-17, 19

pink-spotted ladybug 32-33, 35

longhorn beetle 12-13, 15

longhorn beetle, brown prionid 24-25, 26, 27

longhorn beetle, elderberry 20-21, 23

net-veined beetle 20-21, 23

pleasing fungus beetle 8-9, 11

rove beetle 8-9, 11; 28-29, 30

rove beetle (another type) 28-29, 30

scarab beetle

adult 24-25, 27

larva 32-33, 35

Blue jay 16-17, 18

Bug

assassin bug 20-21, 23

Brochymena bug 16-17, 19

stilt bug 16-17, 19

Bumblebee 8-9, 10; 20-21, 23

Butterfly

American copper butterfly 20-21, 22

comma butterfly 28-29, 31

Page numbers in purple refer to pictures. Page numbers in **black** refer to text.

41

duskywing butterfly — 8–9, 10

giant swallowtail butterfly — 16–17, 18

mourning cloak butterfly

adult — 32–33, 35

caterpillar — 16–17, 18

question mark butterfly — 32–33, 35

red admiral butterfly — 8–9, 10

red-spotted purple butterfly — 12–13, 14

spangled fritillary butterfly — 20–21, 22

spicebush swallowtail butterfly — 12–13, 14

caterpillar (young) — 20–21, 23

caterpillar (older) — 20–21, 23

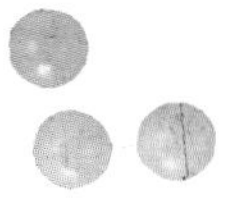

eggs — 20–21, 23

spring azure butterfly — 8–9, 10

wood nymph butterfly — 12–13, 14

wood satyr butterfly — 12–13, 14

C

Chipmunk — 8–9, 10

Cicada

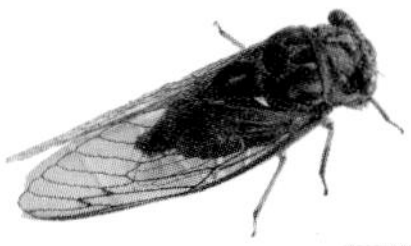

adult — 16–17, 18, 26, 31

adult crawling out of nymph skin — 12–13, 15

nymph skin (empty) — 12–13, 15

Cricket

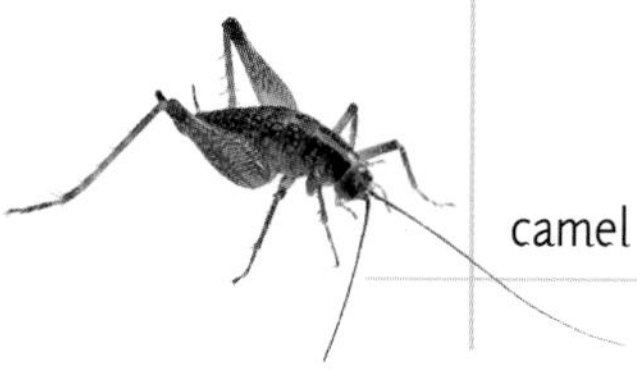

camel cricket — 24–25, 15, 26, 27

*Page numbers in purple refer to pictures. Page numbers in **black** refer to text.*

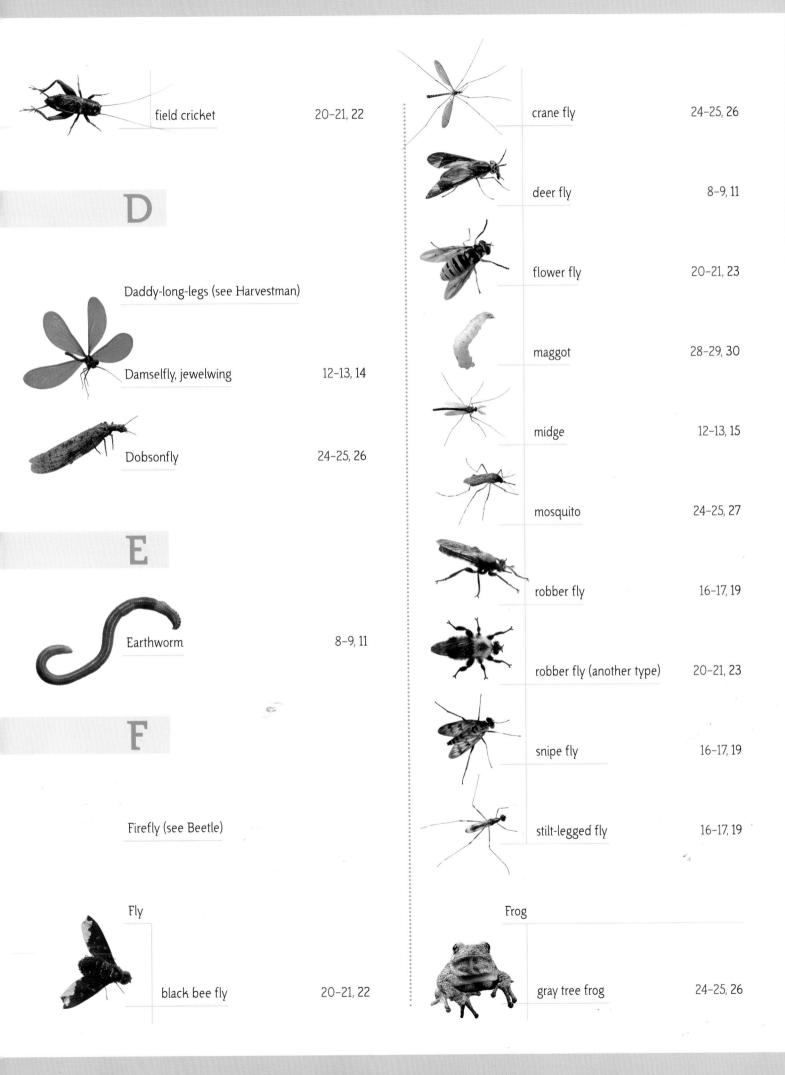

field cricket — 20-21, 22

D

Daddy-long-legs (see Harvestman)

Damselfly, jewelwing — 12-13, 14

Dobsonfly — 24-25, 26

E

Earthworm — 8-9, 11

F

Firefly (see Beetle)

Fly

black bee fly — 20-21, 22

crane fly — 24-25, 26

deer fly — 8-9, 11

flower fly — 20-21, 23

maggot — 28-29, 30

midge — 12-13, 15

mosquito — 24-25, 27

robber fly — 16-17, 19

robber fly (another type) — 20-21, 23

snipe fly — 16-17, 19

stilt-legged fly — 16-17, 19

Frog

gray tree frog — 24-25, 26

*Page numbers in purple refer to pictures. Page numbers in **black** refer to text.*

43

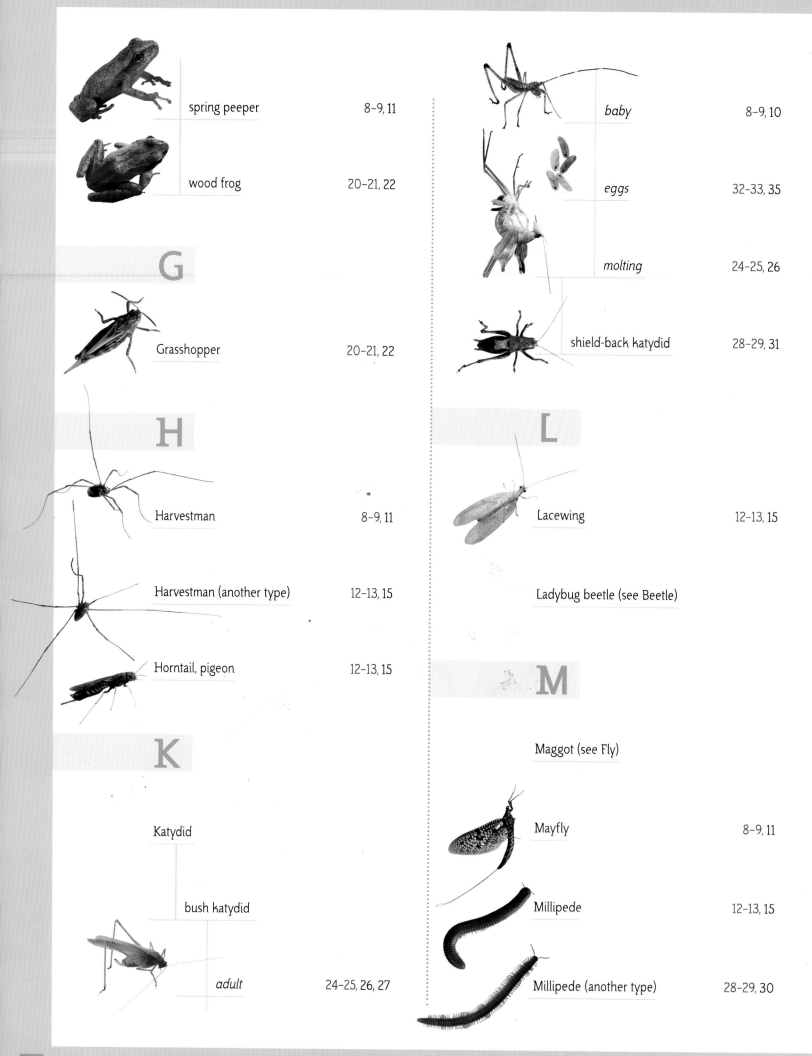

*Page numbers in purple refer to pictures. Page numbers in **black** refer to text.*

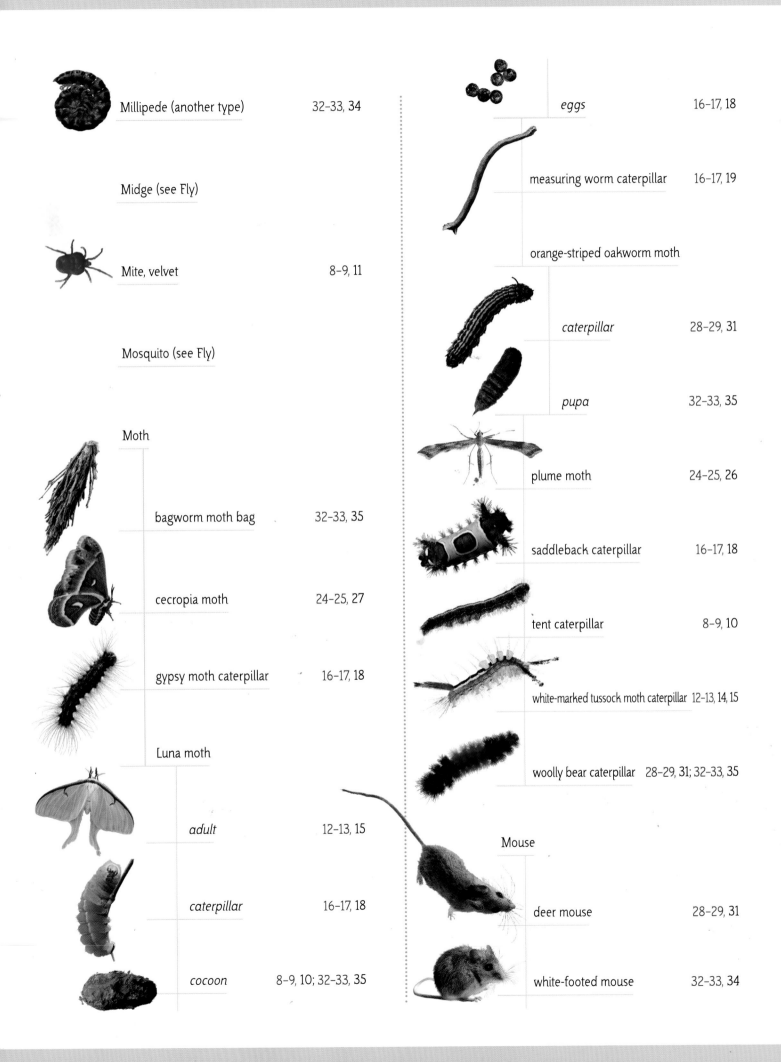

*Page numbers in purple refer to pictures. Page numbers in **black** refer to text.*

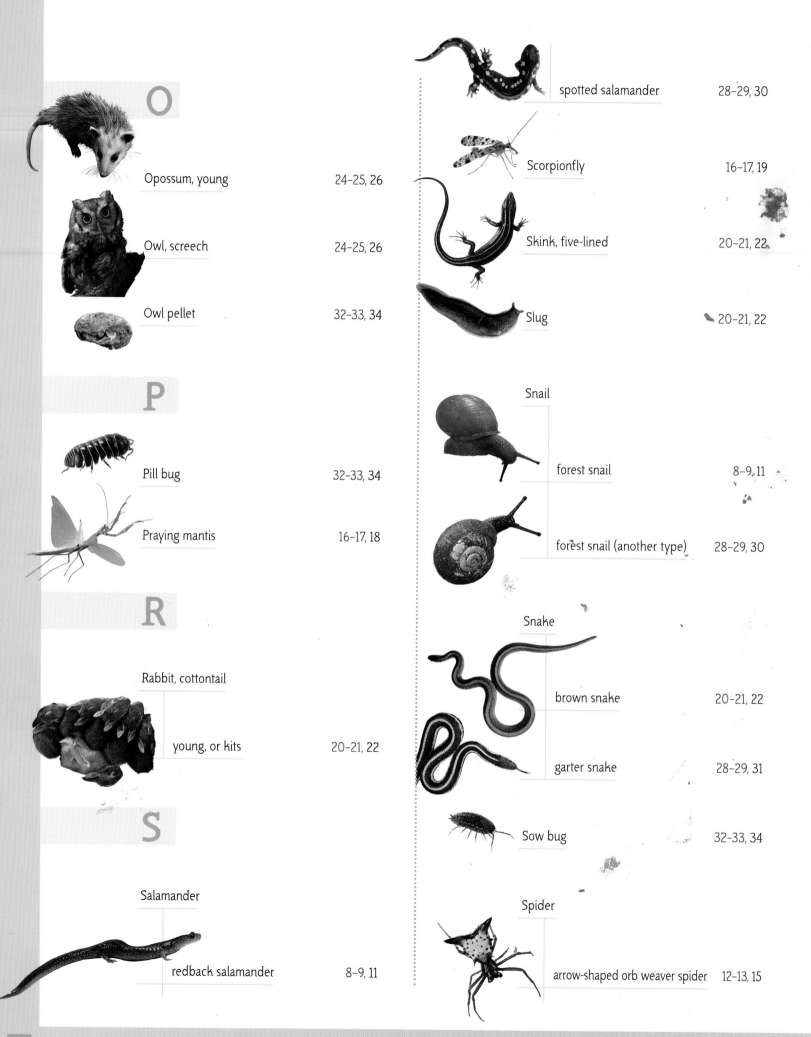

*Page numbers in purple refer to pictures. Page numbers in **black** refer to text.*

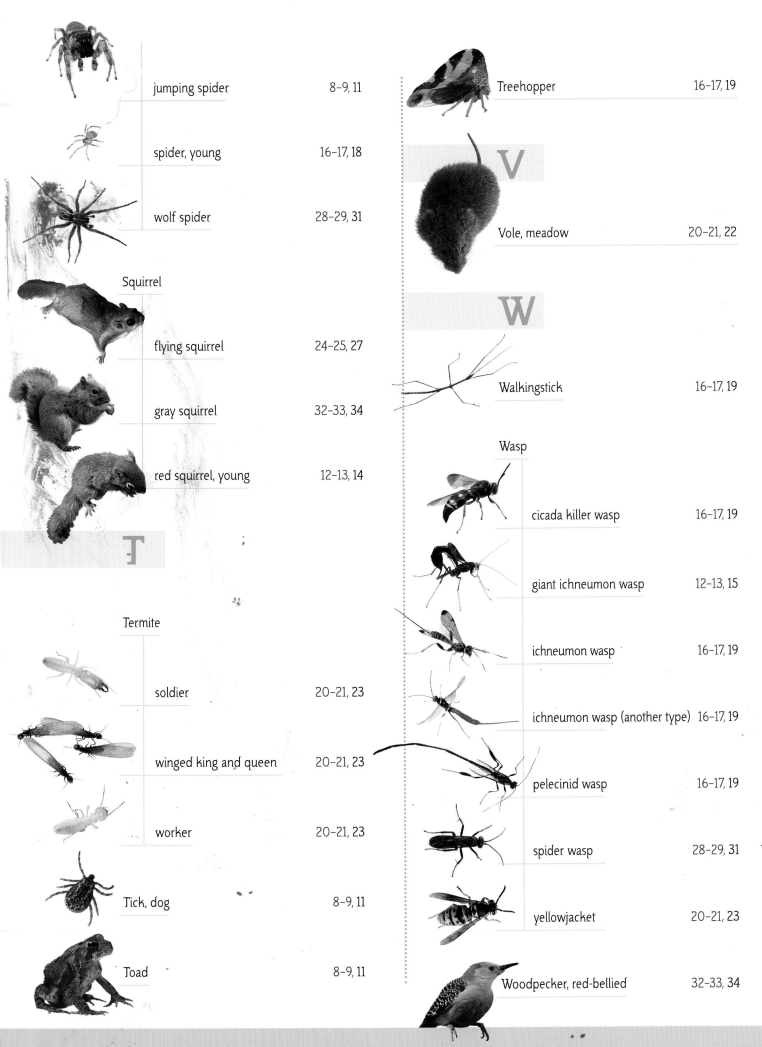

*Page numbers in purple refer to pictures. Page numbers in **black** refer to text.*

About the Photographs

Each large picture in this book is really made of more than sixty different photographs that have been combined to create a realistic illustration. The animals, and many of the plants and other items, were first photographed individually. Then they were scanned into a computer so they could be "cut out" and "pasted" together to build a single picture. Care had to be taken to make sure the final scenes were as true to life as possible. Each photograph was taken with the same lighting to help it look as if everything were photographed at the same time. The animals had to be cut out in the computer very precisely—even each tiny ant—and everything had to have its own shadow created. The flying and jumping animals were photographed using special techniques. To catch the action on film a sensitive laser trigger was used, which tripped a very fast shutter when the insect flew in front of the camera lens. Special high-speed strobes were used to freeze the insect in motion.

Acknowledgments

This book would not have been possible without help and advice from many organizations and people. I wish to thank New England Wildlife Center, New England Alive, Newport Butterfly Farm, Harris Center for Conservation Education, Michigan United Conservation Club, Michigan Department of Natural Resources, Manitoba Department of Natural Resources, Critter Alley, Kalamazoo Nature Center, Lauren Thompson, David Cowan, Nicholas Blacker, Audrey Bishop, Emma, Laura, and Vivien. In particular I'd like to give a special thanks to Bill Westrate, for sharing his firsthand knowledge of and enthusiasm for the small wildlife of this world.

Special thanks to Darrin Lunde, Collections Manager, Department of Mammalogy, at the American Museum of Natural History, for serving as expert consultant on North American wildlife.

Library of Congress Cataloging-in-Publication Data

Bishop, Nic, 1955- Forest explorer: a life-size field guide / Nic Bishop.—1st ed. p. cm. Summary: Depicts in detail several different deciduous forest habitats, with field notes about the insects and animals shown, as well as tips on how to explore a real forest. ISBN 0-439-17480-5 1. Forest animals — Juvenile literature. 2. Forest ecology — Juvenile literature. 3. Forests and forestry — Juvenile literature. [1. Forest animals. 2. Forest insects. 3. Forest ecology. 4. Ecology.] I. Title. QL112.B468 2004 591.734—dc21 2003006553

10 9 8 7 6 5 4 3 2 1   04 05 06 07 08

Printed in Singapore   46
First edition, February 2004

Book design by Nancy Sabato
The text was set in Hattrick, Hunky Dory, and Refield's Lunch.